STARK LIBRARY   NOV - - 2022

CHADWICK BOSEMAN

ACTING ★ SUPERSTAR

MEGAN BORGERT-SPANIOL

Big Buddy Books

An Imprint of Abdo Publishing
abdobooks.com

ABDOBOOKS.COM

Published by Abdo Publishing, a division of ABDO, PO Box 398166, Minneapolis, Minnesota 55439. Copyright © 2022 by Abdo Consulting Group, Inc. International copyrights reserved in all countries. No part of this book may be reproduced in any form without written permission from the publisher. Big Buddy Books™ is a trademark and logo of Abdo Publishing.

Printed in the United States of America, North Mankato, Minnesota

052021
092021

THIS BOOK CONTAINS RECYCLED MATERIALS

Design: Kelly Doudna, Mighty Media, Inc.
Production: Mighty Media, Inc.
Editor: Liz Salzmann
Cover Photograph: Shutterstock Images
Interior Photographs: Ernest Coleman/AP Images, p. 27; Gage Skidmore/Flickr, p. 21; Matt Sayles/AP Images, pp. 15, 25, 29 (bottom); Paul Bruinooge/Getty Images, p. 7; Shutterstock Images, pp. 1, 5, 9, 11, 13, 19, 23, 28, 29 (top); Wikimedia Commons, pp. 17, 29 (center)

Library of Congress Control Number: 2020949949

Publisher's Cataloging-in-Publication Data

Names: Borgert-Spaniol, Megan, author.
Title: Chadwick Boseman: acting superstar / by Megan Borgert-Spaniol
Other title: acting superstar
Description: Minneapolis, Minnesota : Abdo Publishing, 2022 | Series: Superstars | Includes online resources and index.
Identifiers: ISBN 9781532195648 (lib. bdg.) | ISBN 9781098216375 (ebook)
Subjects: LCSH: Boseman, Chadwick--Juvenile literature. | Actors--United States--Biography--Juvenile literature. | Motion picture actors and actresses--United States--Biography--Juvenile literature. | African American actors--Biography--Juvenile literature. | Superhero films--Juvenile literature.
Classification: DDC 791.430--dc23

CONTENTS

Chadwick Boseman ★★★★★★★★★★★★★★★★★ 4

Childhood ★★★★★★★★★★★★★★★★★★★★ 6

Sports & Arts ★★★★★★★★★★★★★★★★★★ 10

New York to Hollywood ★★★★★★★★★★★★★ 14

Black Panther ★★★★★★★★★★★★★★★★★★ 18

Public & Private Life ★★★★★★★★★★★★★★ 22

Death of a Hero ★★★★★★★★★★★★★★★★ 26

Timeline ★★★★★★★★★★★★★★★★★★★★★ 28

Glossary ★★★★★★★★★★★★★★★★★★★★★ 30

Online Resources ★★★★★★★★★★★★★★★★ 31

Index ★★★★★★★★★★★★★★★★★★★★★★ 32

CHADWICK BOSEMAN

Chadwick Boseman was best known for starring in the superhero movie *Black Panther*. Sadly, he died of **cancer** in August 2020. But to his many fans, Boseman will forever be a superhero.

> "If you're willing to take the harder way ... the one with more failures at first than successes ... then you will not regret it."

Before becoming a movie star, Boseman appeared in 14 different TV shows.

CHILDHOOD

Chadwick Aaron Boseman was born on November 29, 1976, in Anderson, South Carolina. He had two older brothers, Kevin and Derrick. His mother, Carolyn, was a nurse. His father, Leroy, worked in a cotton factory.

Kevin (*left*) and Chadwick Boseman in 2018

Chadwick often faced **racism** in the city where he grew up. In spite of this, he had a happy childhood. He looked up to his brother Kevin. Kevin was a dancer. He inspired Chadwick to follow his interest in the arts.

From 2004 to 2008, Kevin Boseman performed in *The Lion King* during its national tour.

SPORTS & ARTS

Boseman went to T.L. Hanna High School. He played on the basketball team. He also wrote his first play. The play was about a teammate who was shot and killed.

Boseman graduated high school in 1995. He then went to Howard University in Washington, DC. He took acting classes and studied directing. He dreamed of becoming a director.

Howard University was founded in 1867. It was one of the first colleges that Black students were allowed to attend.

In 1998, Boseman and other students wanted to attend an acting program at the British American Drama Academy in England. But, they couldn't afford to go.

Actor Phylicia Rashad was teaching Boseman's acting class at Howard. She called fellow actor Denzel Washington. Together, they helped pay for the trip!

SUPERSTAR ★ SCOOP
While going to school at Howard, Boseman worked at an African bookstore.

Rashad is best known for playing TV mom Clair Huxtable on *The Cosby Show* from 1984 to 1992.

NEW YORK TO HOLLYWOOD

Boseman graduated college in 2000. He then moved to New York City. There, he wrote and directed several plays. He also taught acting classes.

In 2008, Boseman moved to California to try acting in Hollywood. One of his first **roles** there was in the TV show *Lincoln Heights*.

The actors Boseman worked with in *Lincoln Heights* included (*left to right*) Robert Adamson, Erica Hubbard, Rhyon Brown, and Mishon Ratliff.

For several years, Boseman acted in different TV series. Then in 2011, he landed an important **role**. Boseman played baseball star Jackie Robinson in *42*. This **biopic** came out in 2013.

In the following years, Boseman acted in other biopics. He played musician James Brown and US **Supreme Court** Justice Thurgood Marshall. But Boseman's most famous role was not a historical figure. It was a superhero!

In 1947, Jackie Robinson became the first Black player in Major League Baseball since the 1880s.

BLACK PANTHER

Boseman first appeared as the Marvel Comics character T'Challa in 2016's *Captain America: Civil War*. T'Challa is the king of Wakanda, a **fictional** African nation. He is also a superhero known as Black Panther.

In 2018, Boseman played King T'Challa in the movie *Black Panther*. *Black Panther* was the first major superhero movie with a mostly Black cast.

In *Captain America: Civil War*, two groups of superheroes fight each other. The leaders of the two sides are Iron Man (*far left*) and Captain America (*far right*).

Black Panther became the first superhero movie to be **nominated** for Best Picture at the Academy Awards. It was one of the most popular movies of the year. And people loved Boseman as King T'Challa!

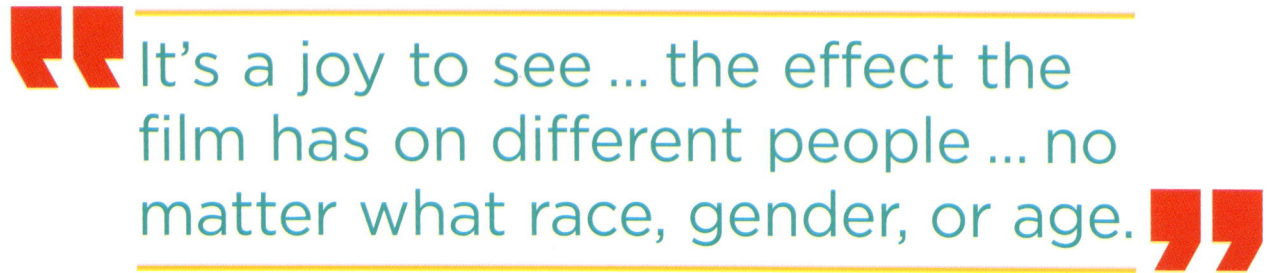

" It's a joy to see … the effect the film has on different people … no matter what race, gender, or age. "

—Chadwick Boseman, on *Black Panther* fans

In 2016, Boseman (*far right*) attended Comic-Con in San Diego, California. He appeared with fellow *Black Panther* stars (*from left*) Lupita Nyong'o, Michael B. Jordan, and Danai Gurira.

PUBLIC & PRIVATE LIFE

Boseman was a new favorite among Marvel fans. He played Black Panther in two more movies. These were *Avengers: Infinity War* and *Avengers: Endgame*.

Boseman took on other **roles**. He was a cop in *21 Bridges*. And he was a musician in *Ma Rainey's Black Bottom*. In February 2021, Boseman won a Golden Globe Award for this performance.

Denzel Washington was one of the producers of *Ma Rainey's Black Bottom*.

Boseman rarely talked about his personal life. But he was often seen with singer Taylor Simone Ledward. They became **engaged** in late 2019 and got married soon after.

Boseman also didn't talk publicly about his health problems. In 2016, Boseman had learned he had **cancer**. He had continued working while going through **treatment**. Few people knew about his illness.

In 2019, Ledward and Boseman attended the Screen Actors Guild Awards together.

DEATH OF A HERO

Boseman lost his battle with **cancer** on August 28, 2020. He died at his home in California. The world was shocked by Boseman's death. In the following days, fans and public figures honored the actor's life. Many likened him to the superhero he played on screen.

> In my culture, death is not the end.

—Chadwick Boseman, as T'Challa in *Captain America: Civil War*

After Boseman's death, a mural featuring him and a young *Black Panther* fan was painted on a wall at Disneyland Resort in Anaheim, California.

TIMELINE

1976
Chadwick Aaron Boseman was born on November 29 in Anderson, South Carolina.

1995
Boseman graduated from T.L. Hanna High School. He began college at Howard University in Washington, DC.

1998
Boseman attended an acting program at the British American Drama Academy in England.

2000
Boseman graduated from college and moved to New York City.

Boseman moved to California to act in Hollywood.
2008

Boseman appeared in *Captain America: Civil War*.
2016

Boseman died of cancer on August 28 in California.
2020

2011

Boseman landed the role of Jackie Robinson in the biopic *42*.

2018

Boseman starred in the superhero movie *Black Panther*.

29

GLOSSARY

biopic—a movie that tells the story of a real person's life.

cancer—any of a group of very harmful diseases that cause a body's cells to become unhealthy.

engaged—promised to be married.

fictional—not real.

nominate—to name as a possible winner.

racism (RAY-sih-zuhm)—the belief that one race is better than another.

role—a part an actor plays.

Supreme Court—the highest, most powerful court of a nation or a state.

treatment—medical care for an illness or injury.

ONLINE RESOURCES

To learn more about Chadwick Boseman, please visit **abdobooklinks.com** or scan this QR code. These links are routinely monitored and updated to provide the most current information available.

INDEX

Avengers: Endgame, 22
Avengers: Infinity War, 22
awards, 20, 22, 25

birth, 6, 28
Black Panther, 4, 18, 20, 21, 27, 29
Black Panther (character), 18, 22
Brown, James, 16

California, 14, 21, 26, 27, 29
Captain America: Civil War, 18, 19, 26, 29
childhood, 6, 8, 10

death, 4, 26, 27, 29

education, 10, 12, 14, 28
England, 12, 28

family, 6, 7, 8, 9, 24, 25
42, 16, 29

health, 4, 24, 26, 29
Howard University, 10, 11, 12, 28

Lincoln Heights, 14, 15
Lion King, The, 9

Ma Rainey's Black Bottom, 22, 23
Marshall, Thurgood, 16
Marvel Comics, 18, 22
movies, 4, 5, 16, 18, 19, 20, 21, 22, 23, 24, 26, 27, 29

New York City, 14, 28

Rashad, Phylicia, 12, 13
Robinson, Jackie, 16, 17, 29

South Carolina, 6, 28

T'Challa, 18, 20, 26
theater, 9, 10, 14
TV shows, 5, 13, 14, 15, 16
21 Bridges, 22

Washington, DC, 10, 28
Washington, Denzel, 12, 23